First Edition

Genuine Autographed Collectible

_____

Do you want me to sign it in ink or in lipstick?

Romantic Poetry From Sharon's Ardent Fan Club

FANS@SharonEstherLampert.com

Gift Card

Date:

To:

From:

Message:

What Do Books Do?
BOOKS ARE POWERFUL!
Books **Educate!**
Books **Enlighten!**
Books **Empower!**
Books **Emancipate!**
Books **Entertain!**
Books **Spring Eternal!**
Books **Drive Exploration!**
Books **Spark Evolution!**
Books **Ignite Revolution!**

Sharon Esther Lampert

BooksArePowerful.com

IT'S NOT EASY BEING A JEWISH SEX SYMBOL

Romantic Poetry From Sharon's Ardent Fan Club

Sharon Esther Lampert
Sexiest Creative Genius in Human History

Literature, Poetry, Beach, Rockaway Beach, Genius, Sharon Esther Lampert

It's Not Easy Being a Jewish Sex Symbol—Romantic Poetry from Ardent Fans

©2024 by Sharon Esther Lampert. All Rights Reserved. No part of this book may be used or reproduced in any manner whatsoever without written permission except in the case of brief quotations embodied in critical articles and reviews.

KADIMAH PRESS: GIFTS OF GENIUS

Books may be purchased for education, business, or sales promotional use.
ISBN: Hardcover 978-1-885872-58-6
ISBN: Paperback 979-8-8689-40-59-0
ISBN: E-Book 979-8-8689-40-60-6
Library of Congress Control Number: 2023924582

Palm Beach Book Publisher, www.PalmBeachBookPublisher.com, Phone: 917-767-5843.
FANS@SharonEstherLampert.com
www.SharonEstherLampert.com

Book Design and Interior Creative Genius Sharon Esther Lampert
Illustrations: Kim Colwell
Editor: Dave Segal
Photography: Dr. Lee, Dr. Rom Roth, Chester Elkind and Avi Rabinowitz

Global Online Websites for Orders and Distribution:
Ingram, 1 Ingram Blvd. La Vergne, TN 37086-3629
Phone: 615-793-5000
Fax orders: 615-287-6990

First Edition

Manufactured in the United States of America

Age 9
THE QUEEN HAS ARRIVED!
"My daughter is a poet, philosopher, and teacher. Sharon is the Princess & Pea!
BEAUTY & BRAINS!"

MOMMY
XOXO

"THE QUEEN HAS ARRIVED!"
—MOMMY

IT'S NOT EASY BEING A
JEWISH SEX SYMBOL

Romantic Poetry From Sharon's Ardent Fan Club

KADIMAH PRESS
Gifts of Genius

Dear Sharon

I haven't any news to write,
So I will merely say,
Because Central (park) was empty
I missed you most today.

Your verse may not be imabic
Of certain men you have bias
But I'd Like you beside me
When I am on that dias.

Of all my new found pals
You must be careful with the pen
Your adroit couplets
Could topple homesapien

Fondly
Jim Marr Jr.
October 17th, 2000

Table of Contents

"Dear Sharon" by Jim Marr Jr.

January: "PHENOMENON" by Harry McVeety

February: "My Man" by Sharon Lampert

March: "Sharon" by Morry

April: "The Scent of a Soul" by Mark Smith

May: "Dear Sharon" by Richard P

June: "To My Light" by Charly

July: "Dear Sharon" by Ari

August: "In Your Words" by Richard S.

September: "Love Has No Boundaries" by Dave

October: "I See a Queen in My Dreams"

By Andre Emmanuel Bendavi ben-Yehu

November: "With You" by Charly

December: "Boris Gudunov in Winter" by Richard S.

January: "What Can I Say!" by Dennis

SEE THE WORLD THROUGH THE EYES OF A CREATIVE GENIUS
KADIMAH PRESS: GIFTS OF GENIUS
FAN MAIL: National & International

FAN MAIL: FANS@SharonEstherLampert.com

Sharon Esther Lampert
Sexiest Creative Genius in Human History

A PHENOMENON...
SHARON ESTHER LAMPERT

Lithe and lovely ... like a fawn.
This lady fascinates me ... from dusk till dawn.
Feminine and comely ... she's beyond belief
A blue-beam from her eyes ... is my soothing relief.

Girlish in her braces ... maidenly in her style
I yearn for her embraces ... and adore her friendly smile.
As tasteful as any artist ... you'll ever see
She's a compendium of class ... from A to Z.

If you'd like to see a figure, that puts Venus to shame
Behold her in a swimsuit, and your passions will aflame.
Ever exuding goodness . . . guided from above
Miss Sharon is the essence, and epitome of Love.

She's the inspiration of sages, and also fools like me
And the most magnificent female, I'm sure I'll ever see.
The nights are now endearing, & never filled with doubt
I sometimes wake up singing, cause it's Sharon . . .
I dream about.

Affectionately,..
A devoted fan,

Harry McVeety

My Man

Making Love All Through the Night and Making Love All Through the Day

For Dr. Jacques Merab

My Man
is passionate and strong, all through
the night—I know his emotional,
spiritual, and physical being; I feel
the breadth and depth of his masculinity

All through the night, **My Man** holds
me tightly in his arms: warm, tender,
and cuddly—childlike—always knowing
where I am, secure forevermore

My Man's touch lingers—
I am sleeping soundly all
through the night, still making
love with him, in my dreams

I awaken to **My Man's** soft kisses at
dawn, my spirit floating in the morning
mist—the promise of love is fulfilled—
my heart is murmuring a melody, a
sweet new song, all through the day

By Sharon Esther Lampert

Sharon Esther's Love Poetry Books:
- 7 Practice Husbands
- One Life, Many Loves
- Epic Love Poem:
  Love Ever Reborn Is Love Ever Newborn
- Sweet Nothings: Love Portraits in Poetry

For My Love, Dr. J.P.M., Harvard M.D., Lebanese-Half Jewish

SHARON

S o, she's tall and blond.
H as big blue eyes.
A nd she's pretty and young (though immensely wise).
R udely I sat. But she talked with me!
O pened her inner mystery.
N ow you know how she cut me down to sighs.

Morry
Sept 10th, 2001

Sharon Esther Lampert
Sexiest Creative Genius in Human History

MARCH PINUP

Photography by Chester Elkind

FAN MAIL: FANS@SharonEstherLampert.com

A poem from a fan
Oct 17, 2013 5:01 PM

Dear Poet, Philosopher, Paladin of Education, Peacemaker, Pioneer, PIN-UP, Prophet, and Princess

I have fallen in love with your website and offer you this poem as thanks

The Scent of a Soul

Crafed and caressed by the hands,
Of a Jewish goddess,
There is a golden jewelry box,
Resplendent with,

Diamonds,
Emeralds,
Sapphires,
Rubies and pearls,

But they are not the true treasure of the box.
For the real pleasure is to take them all out,
And scrratch the red velvet lining underneath,
Which will unlock,

Untold riches of insight for,
The velvet is scented with her soul,
And you will inhale such clarity,
You will wish for nothing more.

Mark Smith

Dear Sharon,

When I'm with you, I see you and nobody else!
The chemistry quickens the beat of my pulse.
Your intellect quickens the pulse of my mind.,
And everyone else is left far behind!
These days till I see you- that's really exciting,
And Saturday night I found something inviting.
It's too bad that Schmaltzy and Felafel can't come,
But I'll bring something for them so that they, too,
can have fun..
So till then, my "Honey," be happy- productive,
And Saturday evening you can just be seductive!
No wonder I'm younger when I think of you --
Your body defies how your mind is so wise!

Richard P.
October 18th, 2000

-To My Light Sharon-

One in Your lifetime, you feel love, once in your time, you know
exactly what it is...

You can find her everywhere, anywhere, anytime, but everything depends
on your persistence if you only want her to be there for you.

I was looking everywhere, smelling every rose, every lilac, every smell
was not the one I was looking for, I was traveling
everywhere, in the big cities of the world, Italy, France, New York,
I said to myself where is my princess, where is my life;

I was in every garden, I was on every rock, I was on every mountain, she was not there as well...

I said to myself this is it, I'm never gone a find the love of my life
I've seen different faces, I been around many people
but no one was the sunshine of my soul...

Until one night, one simple night like the other night,
I felt the most precious feeling and strong energy
in my heart when I saw her for the first time

I knew that was Princess of my Dream I was looking since
I came to his world, I knew by the beauty, I knew by her smell,
I knew in her eyes, I knew by her sound of her voice...

She was the one I was ready to live forever; for her love, for
a touch of her hand, for her smile, for her beauty,
For the look in her eyes, I knew in my soul and in her soul was
only one soul...

To you forever my only true love
I love you
Charlie

P.S. Happy Anniversary, 1 Week Forever and Ever

Dear Sharon,

What a beautiful mind you have!
What beautiful lips your have!
What a beautiful mouth you have!
What beautiful eyes you have!
What a beautiful voice you have!

I wonder if I will have the pleasure to hear you sing in shul.
P.S. I think about you inspite of the fact that you forgot me.

Warmly,
Ari
January 14th, 2002

In Your Words, In Your Voice

Play gently on the stringS
Of my soul, Princess KadimaH;
Each pluck of your fingers. A
Tune from my heart pulls. YouR
Rhyming stanzas from your mind tO
Your hand, to the page, to my braiN

Jump, like bright, mystic firE.
Each word, each feeling, passeS
Wonderously, between two neshamoT.
Each gentle thought, each sigh, eacH
Laughing fancy, comes alivE,
Sends a sign, a connection, drawing neaR.

For Sharon Esther Lampert
Richard Simon

AUGUST PINUP

Sharon Esther Lampert
Sexiest Creative Genius in Human History

Photography by Avi Rabinowitz

FAN MAIL: FANS@SharonEstherLampert.com

Love Has No Boundaries

(Dedicated to Sharon Esther Lampert)
(Nov. 2, 2017)

Is it possible to fall in love from afar.
Without vision, without touch, without smell
An island in the Pacific, a peninsula on the East Coast
It's a tough relationship to sell

But there's definitely a connection
As their phone calls bear out
So they give it further reflection
To try to remove all doubt

She said her life is like a movie
And the cameras are rolling now
Another chapter in her legacy?
She's anxious to see how

Love doesn't always come to those who wait
Sometimes it doesn't come at all.
You wait a lifetime yearning for your beloved
And you end up taking a fall

But sometimes you take a gamble and go that extra mile
You put your fears aside and file away that denial
There's always a risk that haunts at your mind
Whether it's really worth what you may find

A month ago she wasn't even on his radar
But now she's squarely in his sights
So he eagerly awaits her arrival
Through all these countless nights

It won't be long now before they share a big hug
And sweep that uncertainty right under the rug
In the meantime they talk, and write, and do what they can
With the hope it will lead them to the promised land

A wonderful epic this truly would be
As they create their own little piece of history
The script for this story still remains to be written
But just so you know Sharon, I truly am smitten.

Love,
Dave

Sharon Esther Lampert

Sharon Esther Lampert — Sexiest Creative Genius in Human History

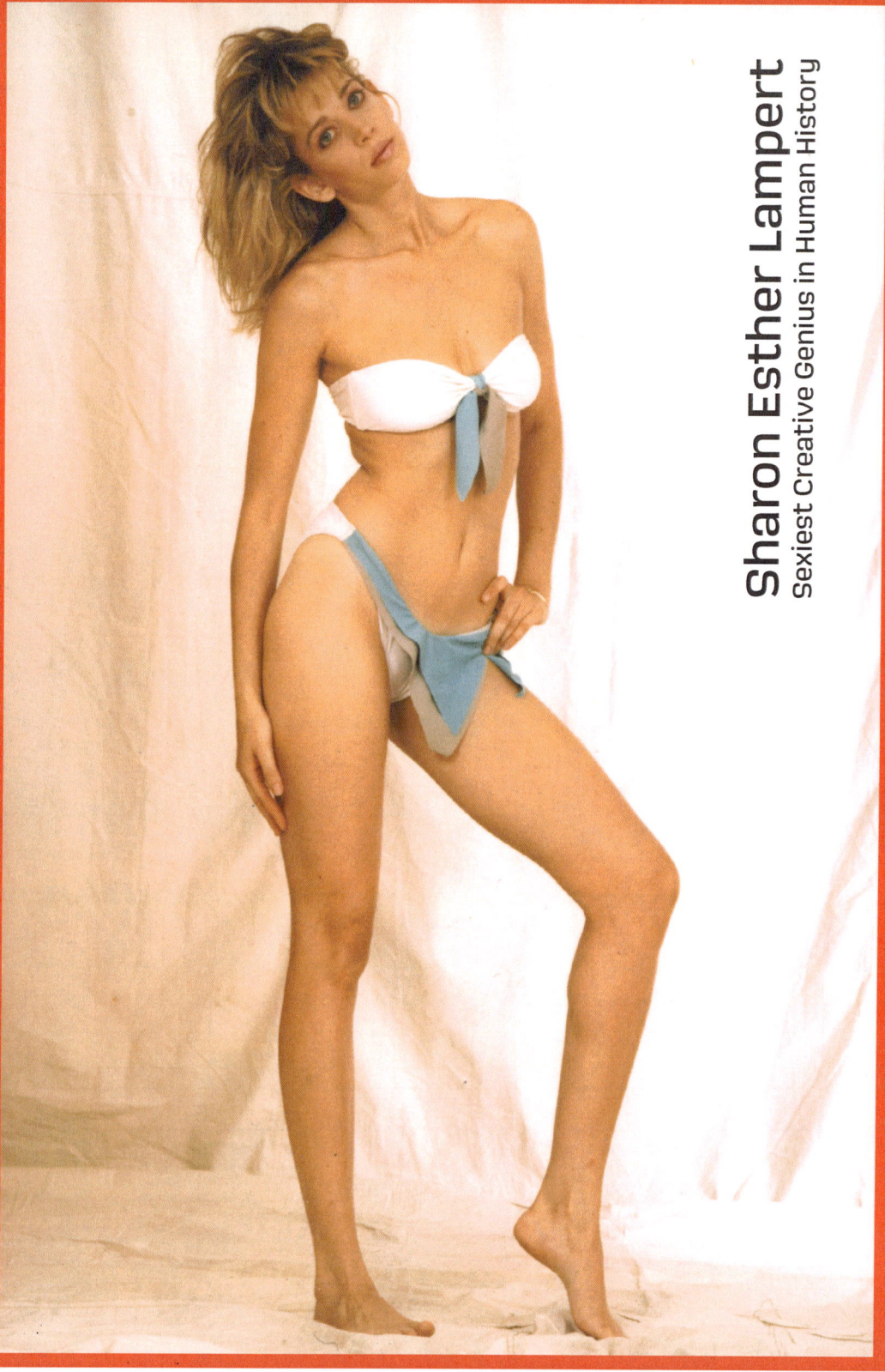

To Kadimah
8TH Prophetess of Israel
Wishing Her Highness a
Properous and Healthy Week

I SEE A QUEEN IN MY DREAM

On the night of the third day of the week I dream...
And I have been dreaming for the last seven weeks.
In my dream... - it is the same every week - seven.
Seven now that I dreamed in the night of the third day!

I saw two infants writing on scrolls with Eagle plumes: "The country whose name is that given by the held angel She shall reign for twelve years pacifying and glorifying"

In turn they wrote, and the elder wrote the first line... It was written on the scroll with a label that read, "NINETEENTH"
The younger wrote the second line on the scroll labeled, "FIFTH,"
And then they copied everything on a third scroll labeled, "TWELFTH."

"She, the glorious queen shall be praised and venerated by kings, "Especially by those producing black gold, one by one shall Live in good co-existing association with the great queen, Whose second given name is that of a great queen of yore"

Andre Emmanuel Bendavi ben-Yehu
4/10/2002

OCTOBER PINUP

Sharon Esther Lampert
Sexiest Creative Genius in Human History

Sharon Esther Lampert

WITH YOU

with you I am myself, with you
I am a smiling sun rising in the morning...
with you my heart is like a sweet
smile of my feelings
with you I go to the end of the world
for you...
with all the beauty of the world
with all the lights in the universe
nothing compares to my love to you...
with you and with you I want
to be forever...
I love you
Charly
May, 2000

BORIS GUDONOV IN WINTER

A swirl of snow and sleet
whips through the bitter cold streets,
as Boris Gudonov
slowly goes mad
in the Kremlin tower.
I hold your hand, warm inside
the theater walls.

It has been the coldest winter,
at every stage;
Will the ice ever melt?
But still,
you are here,
beside me.

When I called you to ask
that we watch Boris tonight, I ponderously warned
"This is not some French confection
Of love and sadness.
This is power and treachery, anger and madness."
"Oh, just like my childhood!"
you sang back,
warming my day with laughter.

I have read you have a genius for
creativity and knowledge.
But I know, too, you have
a genius for
kindness and laughter,
and friendship and warmth;
a genius for
holding my hand.

For Sharon Lampert
Richard Simon
January 27th, 2004

DECEMBER PINUP

Sharon Esther Lampert — Sexiest Creative Genius in Human History

FAN MAIL: FANS@SharonEstherLampert.com

NYU
WOMEN'S VARSITY BASKETBALL TEAM – CENTER

NYC
URBAN PROFESSIONAL LEAGUE – CENTER AND GUARD

KUTCHER'S SPORTS ACADEMY, NY

OMEGA INSTITUTE, NY "BASKETBALL FOR CHAMPIONS"
COACHES:
PHIL JACKSON – CHICAGO BULLS AND BILL WALTON OF BOSTON CELTICS

What Can I Say?

You are unambiguously very interesting,
you sound very intellectual,
you look excitingly pretty
and also...tall.

Nobody can abnegate the fact
that with this plethora of characteristics
you must be,
what I call... a person...gifted!

The only color I like is the color of your eyes
and you are the prettiest...flower I have ever seen.

I am thinking about you all day long.
Excitingly pretty eyes and a smile like an angel.
I am sorry, I made a mistake.
You do not smile like an angel but
I would say that angels smile like...YOU!!

Dennis A
Wed, 19 Jun 2002 23:09:22 -0400

JANUARY PINUP

Sharon Esther Lampert
Sexiest Creative Genius in Human History

FAN MAIL

FANS@SharonEstherLampert.com

Dear Sharon,

You are not only an exquisite poet, you're beautiful! Am smitten by your luminous beingness. Are you an angel in disguise--a so-called malachim in Hebrew if I am not mistaken.

Thank you for your wondeful open-hearted response. **Your photo will sit next to those of Gautama Buddha and the Blessed Virgin Mary.** I will follow your sound esoteric advise regarding the positioning of your photo and the two other icons. I am deeply impressed that you are very conscious about the concept of sacred space and the flow of spiritual energy. So please send me your precious photo as soon as possible.

Happy New Year to you! I am amazed at your tenacity in the act of perfecting your poem about the New York tragedy. **You have the making of a poetic genius.** You've been wrestling with the angel of that poem for the past three months now. I am sure that you'll be able to pin down that stubborn hulk of a poem once and for all. More power and inspiration to you!

Best wishes,
Felix the Cybercat
August, 2001

I asked my brother Benjamin to join me for a modeling shoot. We are three years apart. In our early 20's, we looked like twins. This was a professional-modeling shoot for our portfolio. He quit! I booked a few wedding-dress gigs!

NYC Modeling Card
I booked a few wedding-dress gigs with Blumberg Models

Sharon E. Lampert
772-8601

Hair Blonde
Eyes Blue

Height 5'9½"
Bust   34B
Waist   25
Hips   35
Excellent Legs

Dress Size 6-8
Shoes   8½-9

FAN MAIL

FANS@SharonEstherLampert.com

Tuesday, October 26, 2004 3:22 PM

Hi Sharon,

After having spoken to you on Shabbos, I spied out your website.

It was quite impressive, substantial and unconventional.

I appreciated it more, because I was witness to your passion in our conversation.

A creative genius? It seems you're well on your way.

The sexiest? You bet!

—**Danny**

Darling Sharon,

You are so beautiful.

Please, note how even a plastic straw is affected

by your beauty as it is rising out of the cappuccino!

Love,

Your Muse on Call,

Karl Bardosh (2005)

... Moves me deeply. It's so rare to see such a physically beautiful, and spiritually profound, person on the net.
—AH Aaron Henry

Without a doubt you are the most beautiful person I have ever met, in a spiritual sense, and quite obviously in a physical way too!
Sincerely,
—David

You are not only stunningly pretty but, by judging the little I can read on your works, intellectually gifted. (not a common combination)!
—Ari

Dear Princess,
Thanx for meeting with me.
You are very pretty.
I did not tell you this , but I can see through.
"You have a very gentle and beautiful soul"
A kiss,
—Ari

Never saw I so much beauty all at once.
—Sergio

PRINCESS KADIMAH,
HOW ARE YOU?
HAPPY HOLIDAY: HANNUKAH THE FESTIVAL OF LIGHT AND MIRACLES. HEY, YOU SEEM LIKE A MIRACLE!
—AARON

SEE THE WORLD THROUGH THE EYES OF A CREATIVE GENIUS

- **P**oet
- **P**rophet
- **P**hilosopher
- **P**eacemaker
- **P**rincess & **P**ea
- **P**INUP
- **P**erformer: Vocalist
- **P**layer: Jock
- **P**aladin of Education
- **P**HOTON SUPERHERO
- **P**rincess KADIMAH
- **P**rincess & **P**ea
- **P**resident
- **P**ublisher
- **P**roducer
- **P**sychobiologist
- **P**iano-**P**laying Cat
- **P**hoenix
- **P**rodigy

NYU

Honored Sharon Lampert with an Award for

Multi-Interdisciplinary Studies

(YOUTUBE video)

Sharon was honored to represent her M.A. class at her **NYU** graduation

(YOUTUBE video)

Websites:

SharonEstherLampert.com
PhilosopherQueen.com
WorldFamousPoems.com
PoetryJewels.com
GodIsGoDo.com
Schmaltzy.com
TrueLoveBurnsEternal.com
SillyLittleBoys.com
WinAtThin.com
BooksArePowerful.com
HappyGrandparenting.com
WomenHaveAllThePower.com

PalmBeachBookPublisher.com
MiamiBookPublisher.com
WritersRunTheWorld.com

Education:

Smartgrades.com
EverydayanEasyA.com
BooksNotBombs.com
PhotonSuprhero.com

Artists March to the Beat of a Different Drummer
Sharon Esther Lampert
Marches to the Beat of an Entire Orchestra

Princess & Pea
Sharon Esther wakes up in the middle of the night and writes a whole book.

About the Prodigy
SHARON ESTHER LAMPERT
V.E.S.S.E.L. **V**ery. **E**xtra. **S**pecial. **S**haron. **E**sther. **L**ampert.

PRODIGY
Unleash the Creator, The GOD Within: 10 Esoteric Laws of Genius and Creativity

POET: "A LIST" One of the World's Greatest Poets
WORLD POETRY RECORD: "Through The Eyes of Eve"
The Greatest Poems Ever Written on Extraordinary World Events
http://famouspoetsandpoems.com/poets.html

PROPHET
- The 22 Commandments: All You Will Ever Need to Know About God
- Who Knew That GOD Was Such a Chatterbox **GOD IS GO! DO!**

PHILOSOPHER QUEEN
- Temporary Insanity: We Are All Building Our Lives on a Sand Trap — Written in Letter S
- God of What? Is Life a Gift or a Punishment? 10 Absolute Truths
- Sperm Manifesto: 10 Rules for the Road
- Women Have All the Power But Have Never Learned How to Us It

PEACEMAKER
World Peace Equation

PALADIN OF EDUCATION
SMARTGRADE BRAIN POWER REVOLUTION
PHOTON SUPERHERO OF EDUCATION
- The Silent Crisis Destroying America's Brightest Minds BOOK OF THE MONTH
  - EVERY DAY AN EASY A.com
  - 40 Universal Gold Standards of Education
  - 15 Stepping Stones of Academic Successs
  - 15 Stumbling Blocks of Academic Failure

PIONEER
- SILLY LITTLE BOYS: 40 Rules of Manhood
- CUPID: The Language of Love — Written in Letter C
- Publish: The Secret Sauce of Book Sales — Written in Letter P
- Win At Thin: Fat Me, Skinny Me — Written in Letter A
- SCHMALTZY: In America, Even a Cat Can Have a Dream — Color-Coded Vocabulary Words

The **A**wesome **A**rt of **A**lliteration Using One Letter of the **A**lphabet

PIN-UP
SEXIEST CREATIVE GENIUS IN HUMAN HISTORY

KADIMAH PRESS: *Gifts of Genius*

Poet: The Greatest Poems Ever Written on Extraordinary World Events
Title: I Stole All the Words from the Dictionary
#1 Poetry Website for School Projects
A List: One of the World's Greatest Poets

ISBN Hardcover: 978-1-885872-06-7
ISBN Paperback: 978-1-885872-07-4
ISBN E-Book: 978-1-885872-08-

22 Books of Poetry

Prodigy: WORLD PREMIERE!
Title: Unleash the Creator The God Within
10 Esoteric Laws of Genius and Creativity

ISBN Hardcover: 978-1-885872-21-0
ISBN Paperback: 978-1-885872-22-7
ISBN E-Book: 978-1-885872-23-4

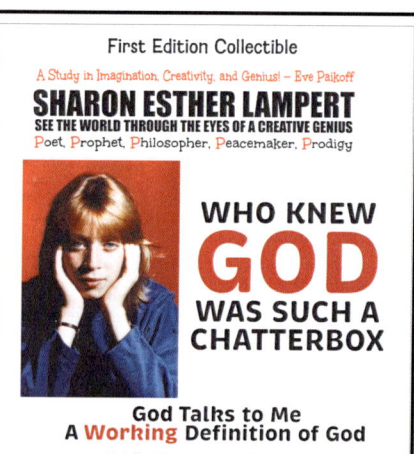

YOU HAD TO OUTDO MOSES!

Prophet: WORLD PREMIERE!
Title: The 22 Commandments
All You Will Ever Need to Know About God
A Universal Moral Compass For All People, For All Religions, For All Time

ISBN Hardcover: 978-1-885872-03-6
ISBN Paperback: 978-1-885872-04-3
ISBN E-Book: 978-1-885872-05-0

Prophet: WORLD PREMIERE!

GOD IS GO! DO!

Title: Who Knew God Was Such a Chatterbox
GOD TALKS TO ME
A WORKING DEFINITION OF GOD

ISBN Hardcover: 978-1-885872-33-3
ISBN Paperback: 978-1-885872-34-0
ISBN E-Book: 978-1-885872-36-4

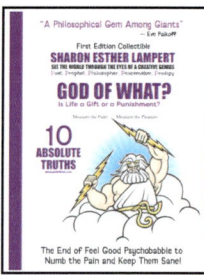

Philosopher: WORLD PREMIERE!
Title: God of What?
Is Life a Gift or a Punishment?
10 Absolute Truths

ISBN Hardcover: 978-1-885872-00-5
ISBN Paperback: 978-1-885872-01-2
ISBN E-Book: 978-1-885872-02-9
GodofWhat.com

KADIMAH PRESS: Gifts of Genius

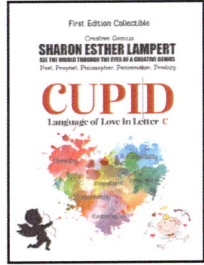

Prodigy: WORLD PREMIERE!
Title: CUPID: The Language of Love — Written in Letter C

ISBN Hardcover: 978-1-885872-55-5
ISBN Paperback: 978-1-885872-56-2
ISBN E-Book: 978-1-885872-57-9
Website: SharonEstherLampert.com

Prodigy: WORLD PREMIERE!
Title: TEMPORARY INSANITY
We Are All Building Our Lives on a Sand Trap — Written in Letter S

ISBN Hardcover: 978-1-885872-70-8
ISBN E-Book: 978-1-885872-71-5
Website: SharonEstherLampert.com

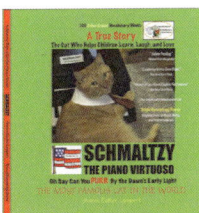

Popular: Children's Book, Ages 8-12
Title: SCHMALTZY: IN AMERICA, EVEN A CAT CAN HAVE A DREAM

ISBN Hardcover: 978-1-885872-39-5
ISBN Paperback: 978-1-885872-38-8
ISBN E-Book: 978-1-885872-37-1
Website: Schmaltzy.com

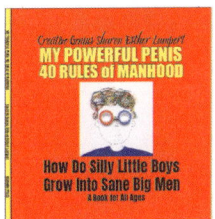

Popular: WORLD PREMIERE
Title: SILLY LITTLE BOYS: 40 RULES OF MANHOOD
HOW DO SILLY LITTLE BOYS GROW INTO SANE BIG MEN?
For Men of All Ages

ISBN Hardcover: 978-1-885872-29-6
ISBN Paperback: 978-1-885872-35-7
ISBN E-Book: 978-1-885872-41-8
Website: SillyLittleBoys.com

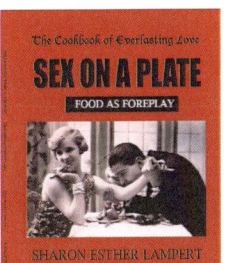

Popular: Every Relationship Begins with a Great Meal
Title: SEX ON A PLATE: FOOD AS FOREPLAY
THE COOKBOOK OF EVERLASTING LOVE

ISBN Hardcover: 978-1-885872-46-3
ISBN Paperback: 978-1-885872-48-7
ISBN E-Book: 978-1-885872-47-0
Website: TrueLoveBurnsEternal.com

I Am Mortal
My Books Are **Immortal**
Please Handle My Books Gently
My Books Are My Remains

This poery book was compiled in one day: July 3rd, 2022
Part 1. Birth — A Selection of Love Poetry from Ardent Fans
More Love Poems will be Published in the Next Edition
Part 2. Format Book — July 3, 2022
Part 3. Publish Book — January 2024

Sharon Esther Lampert
SEE THE WORLD THROUGH THE EYES OF A CREATIVE GENIUS
Poet, Prophet, Philosopher, Peacemaker, Princess & Pea, Prodigy

FAN MAIL: FANS@SharonEstherLampert.com

www.ingramcontent.com/pod-product-compliance
Lightning Source LLC
Chambersburg PA
CBRC101458220426
43661CB00023B/1312